THEN & NOW

EVANSVILLE

OPPOSITE: This is a 1950s view of the first block of Evansville's East Main Street looking west. (Courtesy of Ruth Ann Montgomery.)

THEN & NOW

EVANSVILLE

Ruth Ann Montgomery
and John Ehle

ISBN 978-0-7385-8400-3

Library of Congress Control Number: 2010920194

Published by Arcadia Publishing
Charleston SC, Chicago IL, Portsmouth NH, San Francisco CA

Printed in the United States of America

For all general information contact Arcadia Publishing at:
Telephone 843-853-2070
Fax 843-853-0044
E-mail sales@arcadiapublishing.com
For customer service and orders:
Toll-Free 1-888-313-2665

Visit us on the Internet at www.arcadiapublishing.com

On the Front Cover: This is a 1950s then and a now view of the first block of the south side of Evansville's West Main Street, a busy commercial block since the 1850s. (Then image courtesy of Ruth Ann Montgomery; now, John Ehle.)

On the Back Cover: This is a photograph taken before 1916 of the Baker Manufacturing Company office. Pictured is the sales and office staff, including the company's president, Allen S. Baker. (Courtesy of Ruth Ann Montgomery.)

Contents

ACKNOWLEDGMENTS

The now images in this book were photographed by John Ehle in the fall of 2009. Several institutions and individuals shared their collections of Evansville photographs. My husband, Phillip Montgomery, has been generous with his time in proofreading and sharing his knowledge of Evansville's past.

Unless otherwise indicated, the images from the past in this volume are from the author's own collection. As with the previous Images of America book about Evansville, Declan Every shared his grandfather's, Donovan Every, collection of Evansville photographs (Every). Other photographs appear courtesy of the Eager Free Public Library (EFPL), the Rock County Historical Society (RCHS), and the personal collections of photographs of John and Barbara Willoughby (Willoughby), Jean Petterson (Petterson), Larry Dobbs (Dobbs), Gordon Brigham (Brigham), Richard Luers (Luers), and others as named. All of the addresses in the text are 2009 addresses. Like the landscape of the community, the numbering of houses has changed over the years. A house numbering system used in an early 20th-century city directory was revised when the postal service started door-to-door delivery in the city in 1914. When the 911 emergency system was implemented in the early 1990s, addresses, especially in the newer additions to Evansville, were changed again.

Introduction

The landscape of Evansville, Wisconsin, is constantly changing. This small city in northwestern Rock County is a community that has been in transition since 1839. The arrival of the first permanent citizens brought change to the groves of trees, a small stream of water (Allen's Creek), and rich prairie land.

The trees were used to build the first log cabins along Main Street, Madison Street, and Mill Street. The log homes were soon replaced by frame structures.

Allen's Creek was dammed, and a millrace was dug to power a sawmill and a gristmill. The artificial lake, formed by damming the creek, was named Lake Leota.

In 1900, the dam was removed and the lake was reverted to a stream. In 1923, the City of Evansville purchased the land that had once been Lake Leota, built a new concrete dam, and the lake was restored. It was the center of controversy over the years, as Lake Leota was costly to maintain.

In the 1850s, Jacob West, a brick maker, excavated a narrow strip of clay from beneath the topsoil, shaped it into rectangular blocks, and baked it in a kiln. The new bricks were sold for building houses, churches, and schools.

In the early 1850s, frame and brick commercial enterprises were built along the north and south sides of the first block of East Main Street. Then the commercial district expanded one block west to the first block of West Main Street.

Blacksmith shops, wagon shops, the gristmill, and carpenter shops were built side by side with general stores, hotels, and livery stables.

Residences were built above and next to shops and within a block or two of the business district that expanded east and west and north and south from the corner of Main and Madison Streets. Most homes had their own barns, and some property owners had sufficient land for gardens and fields for crops.

When the Beloit and Madison Railroad proposed a line through Evansville in 1855, more substantial buildings, including a three-story hotel and several commercial buildings, were erected to make the village look prosperous and forward-looking.

In 1855, Evansville's streets were platted. The village was divided into 24 blocks and 11 streets, East and West Main, Church, Liberty, Mill, Madison, Railroad, First, Second, Third, and Fourth Streets.

The railroad did not arrive until 1863, and when it did Evansville merchants and area farmers quickly took advantage of the transportation to commercial and agriculture markets in Chicago. Evansville became a major stock and grain shipping area.

The farmers in the Evansville area began to prosper, and in turn the businesses and services offered by the merchants and manufacturers in the village also prospered.

Businesses and social organizations supplied agricultural equipment, clothing, newspapers, postal service, food, medical services, religious institutions, schools, fraternal organizations, and entertainment.

Evansville residents did not hesitate to raze or move a building if it was in the way of a newer project. House and building movers were in great demand in the late 1800s and early 1900s. Small, older homes were replaced by larger homes built along the residential streets.

The commercial buildings along East and West Main Street were remodeled, razed, and replaced with newer structures built of brick and concrete.

House styles changed, and some families outgrew their residences. Sometimes remodeling was chosen as the best option rather than building or purchasing a new residence.

Additions were made to existing houses. Roofs, porches, and windows were frequently replaced or redesigned. Over the years, siding styles changed and stucco, asbestos, aluminum, and vinyl siding replaced wood on older homes and businesses.

The continual building and changing of the landscape provided ample opportunities for architects, carpenters, masons, and laborers to work in Evansville and the surrounding area. Jacob West, Benjamin Hoxie, William Libby, William Morgan, and William Meggott—all 19th- and early-20th-century builders—are responsible for many of the buildings in Evansville's landscape. Lumberyards, brickyards, and cement manufacturers prospered during peak building periods.

The automobile brought greater mobility and independence from railroad service, and thus the landscape of Evansville again changed.

Fewer grocery stores, lumberyards, restaurants, drugstores, hotels, gas stations, theaters, trains, and other commercial enterprises were noticeable changes in the community over the last 50 years.

The greater mobility of the population brought new demands, as more residents worked in distant cities. There were new demands for apartment complexes, more schools, and government services.

Buildings that housed the former commercial enterprises were adapted for use by service providers. Automobile travelers demanded better roads and more parking lots.

Despite changes to the landscape, the past is always present in Evansville. In 1978, much of the 1855 original plat of Evansville was designated as the Evansville Historic District by the National Park Service's National Register of Historic Places.

With this designation, there was a renewed interest in preserving and honoring the work of the architects and builders of Evansville's homes and businesses. Building owners received state and local awards for renovation of buildings, and craftsmen took pride in the restoration of historic Evansville.

Master carpenters with renovation skills are in demand by commercial and residential property owners. House and commercial building painters have found work in restoring the exterior paint colors to 19th- and early-20th-century buildings.

The City of Evansville has joined the business community in supporting restoration activities. The Historic Preservation Commission provides advice about restoration and preservation. Educating the community about the history of the buildings and preservation is an important mission of the commission.

Within the last 15 years, great care has been taken to build additions to the Eager Free Public Library and city hall that are sensitive to the historic architecture of the buildings. The brick streets on Main Street, from First Street to Railroad Street, first paved in 1914, have been restored.

CHAPTER 1

East Main Street

Evansville's East Main Street was bustling with activity when this photograph was taken before 1904. The first stores were built in the first block of East Main Street. Evansville's Main Street was the trading center not only for the village, but for the farming community surrounding Evansville.

In the early 1900s, Evansville's East Main Street was a model of an early-20th-century business district. Financial, commercial, and entertainment enterprises operated on the north side of the first block. From left to right are the Bank of Evansville, a grocery, Gillman's clothing, Biglow's Furniture and Undertaking, Shiveley's block, Ballard Jewelry, and the Magee Opera House. Union Bank and Trust now occupies the first three buildings on the left; the Magee Opera House was razed.

A mix of commercial space, apartments, and club rooms for social organizations was found on East Main Street when the photograph was taken before 1904. The large block of two-story buildings on the right was razed or moved in 1904. The dismantling of the wood-frame buildings included the remains of the earliest Methodist church. In 1904, William Meggott designed and supervised the building of the Eager block, shown in the 2009 photograph. (Then image courtesy of Willoughby.)

Established in 1870, the Bank of Evansville was Evansville's first bank. Lloyd T. Pullen's general store on the northeast corner of Main and Madison Streets was remodeled for the bank. The bank became Union Bank and Trust in the 1930s. It was remodeled in 1951–1952. The architect was Marlow Ihling of the firm A. Moorman and Company of Minneapolis. Martin Roth of Mauston, Wisconsin, was the contractor. The building used a brown granite foundation and Hebron, North Dakota, brick.

For many years after the Great Depression, Union Bank and Trust Company was Evansville's only bank. In 1968, an addition doubled the size of the building. The store at 4 East Main Street was razed. It had been a theater, a grocery store, a pool hall, and a liquor store. The 1968 photograph shows the store being torn down to make way for the bank expansion visible in the now photograph. Roth Brothers of Mauston was the general contractor. (Then image courtesy of Luers.)

The extension of the Union Bank and Trust Company in 1968 was followed in 2000 by another expansion. The bank purchased the building at 6 and 8 East Main Street, the Snashall and Mygatt building that had been a hardware store, clothing store, and tavern. The building was gutted, and new bank offices and a large meeting room were added. Only the restored 1897 facade of the Snashall and Mygatt hardware store remained.

Jacob West, one of Evansville's earliest settlers, first owned the land at 10 East Main Street. When West built his store, it was one of three general stores in Evansville. In 1848, West's building served as the site of the first post office. After various owners, Walter F. Biglow purchased the store as a furniture store and funeral parlor. The early photograph appeared in the 1900 brochure "Glimpses of Evansville." It has recently been office space.

Built in 1885, the three-story structure at 16 East Main Street, known as the Copper Front Building, was photographed for the 1900 "Glimpses of Evansville." The owner, Marshall Fisher, was a successful real estate agent. The second story was Fisher's office. He shared space with Fred Janes's law office. The first floor was a jewelry store operated by Ernest Ballard and later by Joseph Straka and his son Rowland. Since the 1970s, the first floor of the building has been a beauty salon.

The early photograph, taken after 1904, shows a major renovation of the south side of the first block of East Main Street. On the right at 1 East Main Street is the Pioneer Drugstore owned by Dr. John M. Evans Jr. Today it is a real estate office. The Eager Building at 5–9 East Main Street, second from the right, was The Economy, a department store. Twice ravaged by fire, the Eager Building is rented for offices, retail businesses, and apartments. (Then image courtesy of Willoughby.)

The 1877 construction of the building at 11 East Main Street was a joint venture between Byron Campbell and Evansville's Masonic Lodge. Campbell's brother-in-law, William Libby, was the carpenter. Daniel Huckins did the brickwork. The first floor of the building has served as a post office, picture framing store, bank, Gamble Store, and clothing store. Today it is a heating and air-conditioning business. The upper story was Evansville's Masonic Lodge until the 1920s before being remodeled into an apartment.

From left to right in the 1960s photograph of the south side of East Main Street is the Legion Lounge at 19 East Main Street, Jim's Barbershop at 17 East Main Street, a grocery at 15 East Main Street, the Gamble Store at 11 East Main Street, and the Ben Franklin Store in the Eager block. In the 2009 photograph, the facades of the buildings show remodeling of windows and doorways. Renovation for an insurance office at 17 and 15 East Main Street began in 2009. (Then image courtesy of Luers.)

On the left, at 19 East Main Street, is the Grange Store, built in 1876 for the Evansville Mercantile Association. The upper story was a meeting room for the Evansville Grange. The corner store has also served as a recreation hall for teenagers and more recently as the Night Owl, a restaurant and bar. To the right, at 17 East Main Street, is the building rented by the Grange as a general store before they built 19 East Main Street, which is now being renovated.

The Magee Opera House was built in 1880–1881 by George Magee and was used by local organizations and traveling performers for theater productions and other entertainment. The 1968 photograph shows the Magee Opera House as it was being razed. In the 2009 photograph is a vacant lot where the Magee Opera House once stood. The building to the right of the opera house, constructed as a millinery shop for Magee's daughter, is now the Shannon Law Building. (Then image courtesy of Luers.)

The Baker Hardware Store was built in 1893 by Francis A. Baker, his son Bert, and nephew Fred, and they were in business as the F. A. Baker and Company Hardware. The building had room for a butcher shop, laundry, and a large hall for dances and church dinners. Dentists and physicians also had offices in the building. Through the years, groceries, taverns, and printing offices have found a home at 101 East Main Street. It was remodeled into the Baker Block Apartments in 1990.

In the 1960s photograph from left to right are the Dairy Bowl, a bowling alley and bar built in 1946; the Evansville Review Office, built in 1913; a furniture store built as a wagon shop in 1895; and a roller rink built as a garage in 1924. The furniture store was razed in 1966 for a parking lot. Today the only building serving its original purpose is the Evansville Bowl. (Then image courtesy of Luers.)

Residential and commercial buildings mix in the second block of the south side of East Main Street. From left to right in the 1960s photograph are a small insurance office, two one-story houses, a beautician's shop, Heffel Chevrolet and Oldsmobile dealership, Evansville Veterinary Clinic, an apartment building, another small house, and the Baker block. Today the small insurance office has been razed, and the house was removed from the east side of the Baker block. (Then image courtesy of Luers.)

In 1904, the two buildings in the 1960s photograph were purchased by Alfred M. Van Wormer and moved from the south side of the first block of East Main Street to 135 and 137 East Main Street. The following year, a restaurant opened in the two-story building. Van Wormer used the building on the right as a real estate and insurance office. The building at 135 East Main Street was razed. The Allen Creek Gallery now occupies 137 East Main Street. (Then image courtesy of Luers.)

Lindle Apfel's 1898 photograph of East Main Street looks west from Allen's Creek. On the right, the north side of the street, there is a row of wood-frame buildings. The small lumberyard, visible on the left, was one of three lumberyards operating in Evansville. The 2009 view is of the two-story building moved to the site in 1904, and on the right are brick buildings that replaced the wood-frame structures on the north side of East Main Street.

The 1940s photograph looks west from Allen's Creek on the north side of East Main Street. From right to left are a Standard Oil station, roller rink, and a brick building constructed as a wagon shop. The former wagon shop was later used as an implement dealer, a hatchery, and then as a furniture store. It was razed in the early 1960s. The Standard Oil filling station was razed and a house is now on the site. (Then image courtesy of Willoughby.)

This 1960s photograph in Evansville's industrial area on East Main Street looks east from the railroad tracks. On the right are Green Brothers Grain Elevator, Union Implement, and tobacco warehouses. On the left is Brunsell Feed and Fuel, Laufenberg Lumberyard buildings, and East Side Steak House, the former Evansville House hotel. In 2009, the only buildings remaining are the brick Brunsell Building used as an office and showroom for the Nelson-Young Lumberyard and the lumberyard storage buildings. (Then image courtesy of Luers.)

In the late 1800s, Evansville had three lumberyards. This lumberyard on East Main Street started in the 1860s and has operated continuously under various owners. The 1940s photograph shows a lumber shed and office built by Charles H. Wilder in 1885 and remodeled by Vern Laufenberg in the 1940s. The building on the right was used as an office by a construction company in the 1930s. In 2009, both buildings are part of the Nelson Young Lumberyards. (Then image courtesy of Every.)

The Beloit and Madison Railroad reached Evansville in 1863. The railroad became part of the Chicago and North Western Railway Company. The brick structure was built in 1913 as a passenger depot, and the former wood-frame depot was used for freight. The development of the interstate highway system decreased demand for rail service. The Chicago and North Western Railway sold the depot. Today the former depot is the home of Evansville's McKinney-Hatlevig American Legion Post. (Then image courtesy of Willoughby.)

The 1850s Evansville House was a hotel until 1941. A livery business operated on the grounds west of the hotel. In 1924, the livery barn was razed and a gas station was built. Two years later, Union Street was opened, creating an important intersection on Wisconsin's Highway 13. It was an early route from Wisconsin's southern border to the northern part of the state. (Then image courtesy of Fetterson; now, *c.* 1920–1930 image, courtesy of RCHS.)

A fire in November 1988 destroyed the East Side Steak House, formerly known as the Evansville House hotel. From 1941 until the fire, a restaurant and bar occupied the first floor. The second-story hotel rooms were converted to apartments. The owners decided not to rebuild after the fire. The property was purchased by the Francois Oil Company. A building housing a Subway restaurant, Citgo gas station, and convenience store was built on the old hotel site. (Then image courtesy of EFPL.)

CHAPTER 2

West Main Street

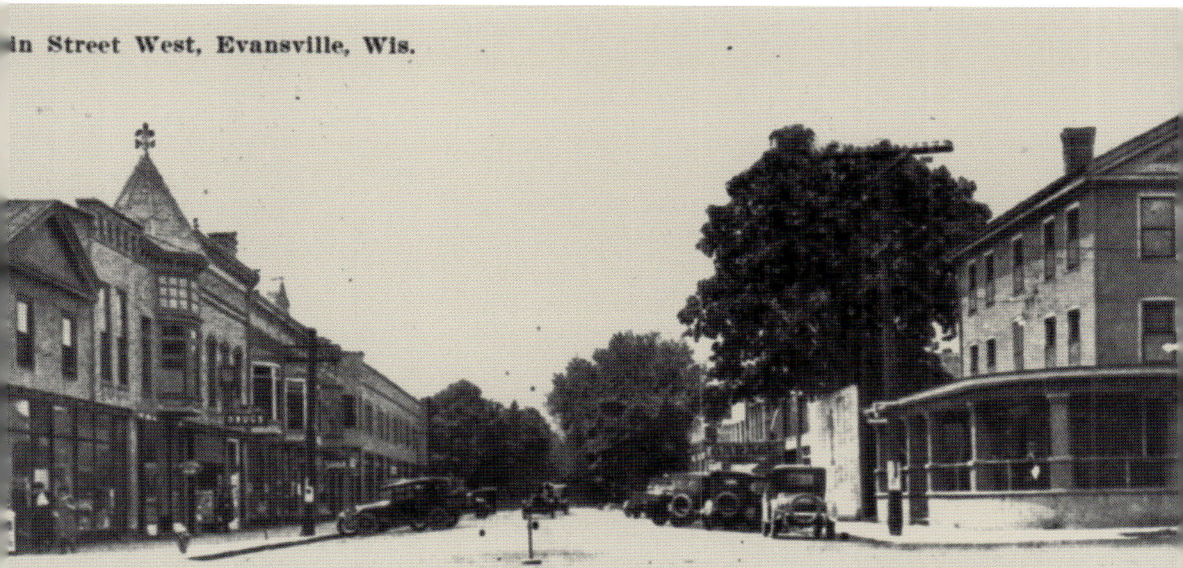

This is a view of the first block of West Main Street in the 1920s, looking west from the intersection of Main and Madison Streets. The corner building on the left and the building on the right were both constructed in 1855 with a hope that prosperity would arrive in Evansville with the Beloit and Madison Railroad.

The south side of the first block of West Main Street was nearly destroyed by fire on September 29, 1896. The fire spread through the row of 13 wood-frame buildings. Heroic efforts, a tin roof, and a brick fire wall on the west end of the structure saved the oldest building in the block, the W. J. Clark store. All of the buildings that can be seen to the right of the Clark store were built after 1896. (Then image courtesy of Dobbs.)

The landscape of the first block of West Main Street has changed many times since the early photograph was taken before the 1914 paving of Main Street with Purington bricks. Looking west from Madison Street, the buildings on the north side of West Main Street have changed due to fires and modernization. The brick streets were restored in 2006. The trees in the photographs mark the beginning of the residential area on the north side of West Main Street. (Then image courtesy of Willoughby.)

The building at 16 West Main Street was constructed in 1870 for Sarah Gunn's millinery shop on the first floor and her residence on the second story. It was purchased by the Eager family in 1900. When Donovan Every took the photograph in 1939, the first floor was a restaurant operated by Ray and Peg Rosen. A fire destroyed portions of the building in 2007. It was restored in 2009 by Christopher Eager and Cheryl Fuchs. (Then image courtesy of Every.)

Evansville's Grange Store was built at 19 West Main Street in 1904 by the Evansville Mercantile Association with William Meggott as the building contractor. Two large department stores thrived in the city, the Grange Store and its East Main Street competitor, the Economy Store. Seven departments, including a bank, grocery, hardware, clothing, furniture, shoes, and crockery were located in the Grange Store. Now the store is rented to several businesses with 19 apartments on the second floor.

In 1900, Eben Reckord built an implement shop at 26 West Main Street. Reckord's family residence was on the second story. This building replaced an earlier wagon shop and implement dealer. A barn north of the shop was Reckord's blacksmith shop. Ray Hyne operated a Buick garage in the building in the 1920s. Hyne remodeled the garage for the Rex movie theater in 1932. An addition was added to the theater in 1941. The Rex Theater operated until the mid-1960s. (Then image courtesy of Willoughby.)

In 1971, the old Rex Theater building was remodeled for an automobile parts store. In 1978, the building was sold to Arnold Willis and Larry Lauke, the owners of the Willis Drugstore. Another pharmacy, the Evansville Pharmacy, moved into the building in 1986. A few years later, the pharmacy moved across the street and a dollar store opened. The building then stood vacant for a couple of years. In 2009, Sew Many Threads occupied the building. (Then image courtesy of Every.)

A house built in the 1850s survived West Main Street's 1896 fire. The house was moved to Madison Street in 1907 to create a site for the Eager Free Public Library at 39 West Main Street. Built in 1908, the library is the newest building on the south side of the first block of West Main Street. A gift of Almeron Eager, it was designed in the Prairie School style by architects Claude and Starck from Madison, Wisconsin. William Meggott was the contractor. (Then image courtesy of RCHS.)

The early photograph was taken after 1951 and shows the new entrance to the Eager Free Public Library that was designed by architect Marlowe Ihling of Minneapolis, Minnesota, and built by Roth Construction of Mauston, Wisconsin. St. John's Episcopal Church is in the background of the early photograph. The 2009 photograph shows the 1995 addition to the south side, designed by architect Mark A. Kraft with construction by Wood, Bauer, and Rather of Madison, Wisconsin. The post office is in the background of the 2009 photograph.

In 1900, Shasta E. Barnard and his wife, Lilla C. Lee Barnard, had a house moved to East Main Street to make a site for their new home at 32 West Main Street. Barnard was a successful tobacco merchant. Shasta and Lilla lived in this home for more than 35 years. Later the house was divided into two apartments, and a two-story sleeping porch was added to the northeast corner of the house. (Then image courtesy of Willoughby.)

One of the most photographed houses in Evansville is located at 44 West Main Street. Its square, steeple-shaped tower and rounded bay windows are unique and have captivated many Evansville visitors. The house was built in 1882 for Byron and Frances Libby Campbell. Frances' brother William Libby was the contractor. This late picturesque stick-style design was readily available in house pattern books of the late 1800s. It was later the home of photographer Elmer E. Combs. (Then image courtesy of Willoughby.)

The Allen-Meredith Funeral Home, at 103 West Main Street, has been both a residence and a place of business. Before Malcolm Allen purchased it as his funeral home in 1930, the house served as an elegant residence, and in an earlier time it was a cooperative restaurant and laundry known as the Evansville Cooperative Home. It is one of the most architecturally significant buildings in the city. It is an excellent example of the Greek Revival style of architecture that was popular in the early 1800s. (Then image courtesy of Every.)

The 1873 drawing shows the home of Evansville's namesake, Dr. John M. Evans (1819–1903). The house was built in 1850. In 1884, Evans razed the house, reported to be one of the oldest in the city. That same year, he built a beautiful High Victorian Gothic–style home using Evansville brick. The Evans home was sold to Evansville's Union Masonic Lodge No. 32 in 1921, and the Masons added a large hall and meeting room in 1922.

In 1893, contractor William Libby built a Victorian house at 114 West Main Street for Dr. John M. Evans Jr. and his wife, May Johnson Evans. After his father's death, the younger Dr. Evans moved next door to the home of his youth. The Carl Brunsell family owned the home at 114 West Main Street from 1912 to 1942. Two Evansville physicians rented the house, Dr. H. F. Smith in 1939 and Dr. Samuel Sorkin from 1940 to 1942 when he purchased the home.

The Richardson family home at 117 West Main Street was built in 1896 for Thomas C. and Amy Porter Richardson, partners in the Grange Store. It is one of the finest Queen Anne–style homes built in Evansville. Their son Lyle and his wife, Hattie Chapin Richardson, lived in the house after they returned from homesteading in Canada. Lyle and Hattie were also partners in Evansville's Grange Store. The home has been in the Chapin-Richardson family for more than 110 years.

The Charles H. and Annette B. Lee Wilder house at 132 West Main Street was built in 1900. It was the third house that Wilder built in Evansville. The Wilder's hired James Wray, a contractor and builder from Janesville, to design and build the house. The Wilder's came to Evansville in 1857, and Charles managed Evansville's first cheese factory and sold cheese to markets in the United States and England. Later he owned a lumberyard on East Main Street. (Then image courtesy of EFPL.)

In 1886, George and Lillian Spencer Pullen built this house at 137 West Main Street. George was an officer at the Bank of Evansville. He also served as the Evansville village treasurer from 1894 to 1896 when Evansville became a city, and he continued to hold the post of treasurer until 1916. The home was featured in *Artwork of Rock County*, published in 1893, and was photographed for the brochure "Glimpses of Evansville," published in 1900. (Then image courtesy of RCHS.)

The Levi and Sarah Leonard home at 138 West Main Street was built in 1868. The Leonard's retired from farming and moved to Evansville to educate Sarah's children, Burr and Marian Jones, at the Evansville Seminary. Burr became a Wisconsin Supreme Court justice. The land north of the home extended to Lake Leota. In the 1880s, Levi and his neighbor Lansing Mygatt created the Leonard and Mygatt subdivision from land north of their properties. (Then image courtesy of EFPL.)

Lansing and Cecelia Mygatt lived in the small house just west of a lot they owned at the northwest corner of Main and Second Streets. In 1893, they decided to build a larger house at 204 West Main Street. His partner in the Snashall and Mygatt Hardware store, Caleb Snashall, was hired to build the house. Lansing Mygatt and Caleb Snashall were two of the six major investors in Evansville's Baker Manufacturing Company.

Three generations of the Winston family occupied this 1850s house at 318 West Main Street. John and Amanda Winston celebrated their 50th wedding anniversary in this house in 1866. In 1901, their son and daughter-in-law, Nelson and Eliza Ann Parsons Winston, celebrated their 50th wedding anniversary in the house. John and his sons, Winston, Reuben and John, operated a general store at the corner of Main and Madison streets. Descendents of John and Amanda Winston owned the house until 1946.

CHAPTER 3

MADISON STREET

For several years after settlement, the Central House Hotel was the only commercial building on North and South Madison Streets. In 1867, the Methodist Episcopal Church was built before the commercial area spread past Main Street into the first blocks of North and South Madison Street. The buildings designed for residences became businesses.

In 1855, Henry G. Spencer built a three-story hotel on this site at 1 North Madison Street. The Madison-Beloit Railroad had promised to build their line to Evansville. Spencer wanted to show the company that the village of Evansville was prosperous, and its citizens were willing to invest in its future. The hotel was a popular stopping place for traveling salesmen and other visitors. It was remodeled several times, including covering it with a stucco finish in the 1920s. (Then image courtesy of Willoughby.)

The Central House hotel was razed in 1937, and the vacant lot was an eyesore to forward-looking businessmen. In 1940, a full-service filling station was built at 1 North Madison Street. The business operated under various owners until the 1970s. The filling station was razed to make room for a new bank. The bank operated under various owners until the Bank of Evansville was built on Evansville's east side. The 2009 photograph shows the office of Roger Roth, CPA.

On the right at 10 North Madison Street was Snashall and Mygatt's Hardware storage. Before it was razed for the Union Bank and Trust parking lot, the small shop also was a milk depot, a laundry for feathers and ticking used in bedding, a feed store, a battery store, a tire store, and Petterson's plumbing and heating store. On the left is a livery stable and partially visible on the far left is a photography studio. (Then image courtesy of Petterson.)

The building on the right was built in 1892 by Ashbel Charles Thorp as a warehouse for his farm implement business. Later Charles Fuller used the building as his livery stable. The building on the left was built in 1893 by Elmer E. Combs as a photographer's studio. The 2009 photograph shows the two buildings at 12 and 14 North Madison Street connected as a single business, Pete's Inn, a restaurant and bar. (Then image courtesy of Brigham.)

The three buildings in the 1900 photograph were residences converted to commercial use. The building on the left was a photography studio for Hattie Spencer, Evansville's first female commercial photographer. The building in the middle was a dentist office. The middle house was moved to Milbrandt Road, and two were razed to expand Evansville's commercial district on North Madison Street. Now an insurance office and bank occupy the site of the three residences. (Then image courtesy of Willoughby.)

The home of William Campbell on North Madison Street was built in 1855 by Nathaniel Libby. It was sold to George Spencer in 1887. Spencer hired Nathaniel's son William Libby to remodel the house. It became a photographer's studio for Spencer's daughter Hattie and a doctor's office for his son George. In 1953, the residence was torn down and the office of the Union Mutual Insurance Company was built on the site. Steve Hagen's insurance office can be seen in the 2009 photograph. (Then image courtesy of Willoughby.)

The home and doctor's office at 34 North Madison Street was built in 1874. Dr. Eugene L. Beebe, an eye specialist, was his own building contractor. The stonework was done by Daniel Huckins and his assistants. Architect-builder Benjamin Hoxie was in charge of carpentry. Hoxie's chief assistant was Andros Munger. The plasterers were Isaac H. Brink and William Taggart. For many years, it was the home and chiropractic office of Dr. Peter S. Kauth. Now it is a private residence.

Josh M. Owen and his wife, Margaret F. Smiley Owen, built this house at 47 North Madison Street in 1903. The couple operated the Commercial House, a popular hotel on East Main Street in Evansville, for more than 30 years. Henry Hogans, a real estate agent, purchased the home in 1920 and lived in it until his death in 1963. The James Cook family has lived in the house since the 1960s. (Then image courtesy of Willoughby.)

In 1935, Howard and Grace Bruce and their son Mark started the Badger Coach Company on North Madison Street. They manufactured small house trailers designed to hitch to an automobile. The trailers had sleeping quarters and a kitchen. The business was successful, and an addition was made in 1940. The Bruce's sold the building in 1963 and subsequently it has housed several businesses, a real estate office, liquor store, restaurant, and video store. Now it is an apartment building. (Then image courtesy of RCHS.)

Baker Manufacturing, organized in 1873, was famous for Monitor windmills and water-pumping equipment. In front of the 1898 cream brick office are the Evansville office staff, managers, and salesmen from Baker's branch offices. The company's president, Allen S. Baker (1842–1916), is the bearded man seated second from the left in the second row. In 2000, the brick building was moved from East Church Street to the corner of North Madison Street and the park entrance tc serve as a museum. (Then image courtesy of EFPL.)

North Madison Street's bridge over Allen's Creek was near the Chicago and Northwestern Railway tracks. In 1931, the Wisconsin Highway Commission financed a new bridge with a 2¢ gasoline tax. The 1931 bridge, known locally as the viaduct, connected Wisconsin Highway 92 with Wisconsin Highway 13, later named U.S. Highway 14. The bridge raised North Madison Street over the Chicago and North Western Railroad tracks to prevent train and automobile accidents. (Then image courtesy of Every.)

The concrete and steel viaduct in the 1930s photograph was a major architectural feature at the northern entrance into Evansville. In 1931, the Whitewater Bridge Company received the contract for it. There were 152 unemployed Evansville men between the ages of 18 and 64 that applied for 50 jobs. It took four months to complete the concrete and steel bridge. The viaduct was removed in 1981, and a small bridge over Allen's Creek replaced it. (Then image courtesy of Willoughby.)

On South Madison Street, Dr. John M. Evans and his son Dr. John M. Evans Jr. built an addition to the south side of their drugstore at the corner of Main and Madison Streets in 1893. The former hospital at 8 South Madison Street was leased to the Wisconsin Telephone Company for 40 years (1926–1966). Since the late 1960s, the first floor of the building has served as office space with an apartment on the second story. (Then image courtesy of Willoughby.)

The 1885 brick building at 11 South Madison Street was the office of the Evansville weekly newspapers, the *Enterprise* and the *Tribune*. The publisher, Caleb A. Libby, was a member of a large family that settled in Evansville in 1855. Libby was a Civil War veteran. After the war, Libby became a pension agent and obtained compensation for the veterans, their widows, and children. Barbershops, art studios, appliance stores, snack bar, photography studios, and hair salons have also used the building.

In 1930, Lester Thompson built a brick Ford dealership and filling station at 16 South Madison Street. Thompson, a Ford dealer in Evansville since 1926, retired and turned the garage and dealership over to his son Donald. The business was sold to John T. Van in 1973. In the early 1980s, Ronald Arndt moved his heating and air-conditioning business into the building. Arndt built a new facility on Water Street and remodeled the building, Arndt Plaza, for office space. (Then image courtesy of Every.)

The 1900 photograph shows, from left to right, the city hall and Methodist Episcopal Church on the west side of the first block of South Madison Street. Both buildings have been remodeled several times. The Evansville Fire Department used two doors on the south side of the city hall. As the equipment changed from horse-drawn steamers to trucks, the doors were remodeled to accommodate the larger equipment. Recent additions for elevators were built on the north side of the church and the municipal building.

Marshall Fisher, an enterprising real estate agent, hired architect-builder William Meggott to construct one of Evansville's first apartment buildings at the southwest corner of South Madison and West Church Streets. The building had two apartments on each floor. The Fisher family owned the home until 1950, when doctors Rodney J. and Roger S. Gray purchased the house for a physician's office. It became a private home after the Grays built a new medical office west of the house. (Then image courtesy of EFPL.)

CHAPTER 4

Churches and City Hall

"Glimpses of Evansville" was designed and photographed in 1900. Evansville's 1892 city hall and the Methodist Episcopal Church are represented here. Each of the buildings has been razed or remodeled. St. Paul Catholic Church, built in 1906, was represented with the other churches in the 1910 Prospectus of Evansville.

The Episcopalians built St. John's Episcopal Church in 1869 at a cost of $3,000. The architect-builder was Benjamin Hoxie. From left to right in the 1900 photograph are the church and the Episcopal rectory, built in 1883–1884 by William Morgan. St. John's Lutheran Church purchased the buildings in 1937 and sold the church to H. Fred Brunsell in 1958. The church was razed in 1959 to build Evansville's post office. Now the rectory, at 20 South First Street, is a private residence.

Evansville's oldest church building is located on the south side of the first block of West Church Street. The wood-frame structure was built in 1854 for the Free Will Baptist congregation. A bell tower, including a new north side entrance, was added in 1899. In early 1914, the Free Methodist congregation purchased the church. Today the Grace Independent Baptist congregation holds services in the church. The pastor and his family live in the rectory west of the church.

The Methodist Church in the first block of South Madison Street was built in 1867. It was the second church that the congregation built. The first was on East Main Street in the middle of the commercial district. The old church was remodeled into stores and razed in 1904. The church on South Madison Street was enlarged in 1956–1957 with an addition for Sunday school rooms. In 2009, the congregation added an accessible entrance on the north side of the building. (Then image courtesy of Willoughby.)

The Baptist Church was organized in 1856. A small brick church was built at the southwest corner of Church and South First Streets in 1867. In 1903, the old church was razed. Caleb Snashall, a hardware merchant and house builder, was the architect-builder for the new church. Snashall died several months before the church was completed. Today the Oak Grove congregation occupies the church. It has some of the most beautiful stained-glass windows in the city.

The early photograph, taken before 1902, shows the Congregational United Church of Christ, built in 1857, at the corner of South First and Church Streets. In 1902, the tower was raised 20 feet higher, and an addition was made to the west side of the building. The 2009 photograph shows the church with its last major addition made in 1963–1964 on the west side of the church for Sunday school rooms. This addition was the gift of H. Fred Brunsell.

The early photograph of St. Paul Catholic Church was taken before 1913, when the tower was remodeled. William Meggott designed the church, which was built in 1906. In September 1907, ground was broken for a rectory south of the church, shown on the right in each photograph. The contractor was Arford Jones. A new rectory on the east side of the church was purchased in 1922. The old rectory is now used as rental property and occasionally as a parish office.

Evansville's city hall was built in 1892, four years before Evansville adopted a city form of government. The building was designed by Conover and Porter of Madison. D. W. Worth, of Baraboo, was the mason. The cream brick was purchased from brickyards in Jefferson, Wisconsin. The village board awarded Benjamin Hoxie the contract for carpentry and finish work on the building. Originally built to hold all city offices and equipment, the police and fire departments now have separate buildings.

CHAPTER 5

Buildings of Historic Interest

This is part of a collage of Evansville Streets from a page in the 1900 promotional brochure "Glimpses of Evansville." Evansville residents were proud of their tree-lined streets, schools, and commercial and residential buildings. In 1896, Evansville was incorporated as a city, and by 1900 there were 1,900 residents.

On the right is the Evansville Seminary, a private school, built in the late 1850s by the Methodist Church. In 1880, the Free Methodists purchased the seminary. The building on the left was constructed in 1888, with William Libby as the contractor. Both buildings were used by the Wyler School from 1928 to 1979. Now the buildings, including the seminary's gymnasium that was constructed in 1916, are the Seminary Park Apartments. Towers have been removed and an entrance with an elevator addition connects the two buildings.

The residence at 218 North Fourth Street was a farmhouse built in the 1800s. In the 1880s and 1890s, the farm was owned by Peter Aller. In 1887, Aller became superintendent of the Rock County Insane Asylum and Poor Farm in Johnstown and later Janesville. He sold the farm to Wellington Smith, and later Dr. Fred Colony owned the farm. Fred Rodd purchased Colony's land and an adjoining farm before 1917. The Rodd-Every family continues to own the property. (Then image courtesy of Every.)

John and Sarah Andrews purchased the home at 262 West Church Street in 1868. All five of the Andrews children attended the Evansville Seminary. Sarah's father, William Wright, planted many species of trees on the property, including maple, elm, apple, walnut, butternut, and pine. The home remained in the Andrews family for more than 80 years. More recent owners remodeled the house and made an addition to accommodate a bed-and-breakfast business. Now it is a private residence. (Then image courtesy of EFPL.)

RESIDENCE OF A. S. BAKER.

Allen S. and Margaret Baker built this home at 39 West Liberty Street in 1883. An older house was moved to a lot on South First Street to build the new residence. Allen S. Baker was an inventor of engines and windmills. As president of the Baker Manufacturing Company, he promoted industrial development and public utilities, including electricity, a public water system, and a telephone company for Evansville. More recent owners have changed the design of the porches.

The home of Benjamin S. and Ellen Woodbury Hoxie at 409 South First Street was built in 1884. Hoxie submitted the design and an essay about the interior and exterior construction to *Carpentry and Building* magazine for publication in the February 1889 issue. The home was purchased in 1906 by Hoxie's daughter and son-in-law, Eva and Everett Van Patten. Descents of the Hoxie family lived in the house until Lulu Van Patten went to a nursing home in the 1970s.

The home at 227 West Church Street was designed and built by Benjamin S. Hoxie for Ellen S. Biglow in 1886. Charles J. Pearsall, manager of Evansville's D. E. Wood Butter Company, and his wife, Harriet, purchased the home in 1898. The Pearsalls moved the small house, shown in the early 1900s photograph, to Liberty Street and created a larger yard for their three sons and a daughter. The large barn in the 2009 photograph is typical of many barns in Evansville's historic district. (Then image courtesy of EFPL.)

The home of Caleb and Mary Isabella "Belle" Shurrum Lee at 23 South First Street was built in 1889. After their marriage in February 1889, Lee made the drawings for the new house and planned to superintend the work himself. Caleb and Belle hired architect-builder Benjamin S. Hoxie to add the finer architectural details to the house plans and to apply his skillful workmanship as master carpenter. Typical of many of the large, older homes in Evansville, it was remodeled into two apartments.

Marshall Fisher, a real estate agent, built this house at South Second Street in 1893. The house is in the Hunt addition to Evansville. In addition to the house, Fisher purchased 9 acres for speculation. The early photograph was taken in 1899 after Fisher had a new veranda and corner window built on the house. In the 2009 photograph, the veranda has been enclosed and the corner window is still visible on the southeast corner of the house.

Before 1893, property owners on Main Street and Montgomery Court owned undivided land that extended north from their residences. After a bitter legal battle with the landowners, the Village of Evansville paid each property owner a settlement and opened Garfield Avenue for residential development. Residential building began immediately. The settlement and increased property values benefited the property owners. Some of Evansville's finest homes were built in the first two blocks of Garfield from 1893 to 1915.

One of Evansville's 19th-century carpenter-builders, William Libby, built this house in 1895 as his own home. He first built a barn on the property and during the summer of 1895 lived in the barn until the house was finished a few months later. The early photograph was taken in the late 1930s, when Erwin Gabriel, a real estate agent, owned the house. In more than 110 years, the exterior of the house has been altered only slightly. (Then image courtesy of Every.)

The home of Seymour Purinton and his wife, Ann Tryphena Jones Purinton, was at 119 Garfield Street. It was built in 1912. Oscar Lehnherr owned the home when the early photograph was taken in the 1930s. On the left of the 2009 photograph is a one-story addition to the house. The screened porch on the front of the house has also been removed. (Then image courtesy of Willoughby.)

Charles E. Cummings, a partner in the Cummings and Clark General Store, built this beautiful Queen Anne–style home at 120 Garfield Avenue. The photograph was taken in 1898 for an Evansville promotional brochure printed by the weekly newspaper, the *Tribune*. For many years, it was the home of jewelry store owners Rowland and Terry Straka. It remains a single-family residence owned by Roger and Kathy Roth.

Fred and Jessie Howard Gillman, along with their daughter Cleve and son in-law Forrest Durner, built the duplex at 123–125 North First Street in 1916. H. O. Walton was the contractor. John Hanson was the mason. Fred was Evansville's chief of police and owned a men's clothing store with his father and brother. Forrest was a director of the Farmers and Merchants Bank, which later merged with Union Bank and Trust. Restoration in 2009 included new siding and porches. (Then image courtesy of David S. Fellows.)

In 1910, Vivus C. Holmes built one of Evansville's last large Victorian homes at 443 South First Street. Holmes was a partner in the large department store owned by the Evansville Mercantile Association, known as the Grange. William and Jenny Bone purchased the house in 1934 for the Leota School for Girls. When the Leota School closed in 1959, Jenny Bone sold the house, and the succeeding owners have used it as a private residence.

www.arcadiapublishing.com

Discover books about the town where you grew up, the cities where your friends and families live, the town where your parents met, or even that retirement spot you've been dreaming about. Our Web site provides history lovers with exclusive deals, advanced notification about new titles, e-mail alerts of author events, and much more.

MADE IN THE USA

Arcadia Publishing, the leading local history publisher in the United States, is committed to making history accessible and meaningful through publishing books that celebrate and preserve the heritage of America's people and places. Consistent with our mission to preserve history on a local level, this book was printed in South Carolina on American-made paper and manufactured entirely in the United States.

This book carries the accredited Forest Stewardship Council (FSC) label and is printed on 100 percent FSC-certified paper. Products carrying the FSC label are independently certified to assure consumers that they come from forests that are managed to meet the social, economic, and ecological needs of present and future generations.

FSC
Mixed Sources
Product group from well-managed forests and other controlled sources

Cert no. SW-COC-001530
www.fsc.org
© 1996 Forest Stewardship Council

Find Your Place in History.